A Great Little Cajun Book
A Gift From Louisiana

EDITED BY: Jeanne Verlenden and Dee Danaher

A GREAT LITTLE CAJUN BOOK has wonderful Louisiana recipes that are common to the Cajun cooking experience. We've chosen recipes that the new or experienced cook can enjoy preparing with ease! So, fire up the oven, get out the big black pot, & let the good times roll!!

D1809578

SOUTHERN FLAVORS PUBLICATIONS
P. O. Box 922
Pine Bluff, Arkansas 71613

Copyright 1992

SOUTHERN FLAVORS, INC.

First Printing, January, 1992
Second Printing, November, 1992
Third Printing, September, 1995

Please use order form in the back of book to order **A GREAT LITTLE CAJUN BOOK** and other Southern Flavors Publications.

WATCH FOR OTHER PUBLICATIONS FROM SOUTHERN FLAVORS, INC.

ISBN 0-9618137-5-X

Printed by
Favorite Recipes® Press   P.O. Box 305142   Nashville, Tennessee 37230
1-800-358-0560

LAISSEZ LE BON TEMPS ROULER!!

For the Cajuns of Louisiana, "il n'y a pas de sauce qui egale l'appetit" could be the definitive statement of their culture!! In English, it means "there is no sauce like appetite!" And appetite is the only prerequisite, along with a big, black pot, for enjoying Cajun Cooking!

Thus, when we think of Louisiana, we immediately think of good food shared with good friends and family resulting in the very best of good times! Our little book brings recipe favorites from Cajun Country to you and your friends and neighbors! You _all_ will love the gumbos, jambalayas, and etouffees along with the traditional favorite recipes that make Louisiana cooking so deliciously distinctive!!

From appetizers to desserts, we have selected Cajun recipes that are fun to prepare and that guarantee no leftovers!! So, enjoy, and "laissez le bon temps rouler!!" (LET THE GOOD TIMES ROLL!!)

Jeanne Verlenden   Dee Danaher

Southern Flavors, Inc.

Copyright 1992
All rights reserved.

Contents

Contents (continued)

Today's Cajuns are descendants of the Acadian French who, in the late 18th century, migrated from Canada to South Louisiana. Cajuns all have one great love - food, and Cajun Country is where it is King!!

SUPER CAJUN CHEESE BALL

2 (8 oz.) pkgs. cream cheese
1 stick butter
5 garlic pods, crushed
1 bunch green onions & tops,
 chopped
1 (2-1/2 oz.) jar dried beef, chopped
1 cup pecans, chopped
2 Tbsps. parsley, chopped for
 garnish

Combine ingredients well; shape into ball; chill 3-5 hours or overnight. Before serving, garnish with parsley; serve with Ritz, rye, and sesame crackers. Pretty served at Christmas garnished with holly! Wonderful!

Fresh garlic is the mainstay of many Louisiana dishes!

LOUISIANA SCRAMBLE

1 pkg. each Good Seasons Blue
 Cheese, Italian, & Cheese Garlic
 Salad Dressings
1 (2-1/4 oz.) bottle capers, drained
2-3 onions, sliced in rings
2-3 lbs. shrimp, cooked & peeled
2 (4 oz.) cans whole button
 mushrooms, drained
2 (14 oz.) cans artichokes, drained
Salt & red pepper to taste

Prepare dressings per packages' directions, but OMIT WATER AND REPLACE WITH VINEGAR. In deep bowl, combine dressings and rest of ingredients; marinate overnight. Stir occasionally. Colorful served in big glass bowl with toothpicks for "spearing."

Serves 20.

*A Great Little Cajun Recipe
Just For You!*

To:

FRENCH QUARTER BEIGNETS

2 cups all purpose flour
1/2 tsp. salt
1 Tbsp. baking powder
1 tsp. ground cinnamon
1 egg, beaten well
3 Tbsps. sugar
1 cup milk
1/2 tsp. vanilla extract
Hot oil for deep frying
2 cups powdered sugar

Into bowl, sift first 4 ingredients. Separately, beat well egg with next 3 ingredients; pour into flour mixture; stir until moistened. Turn onto floured surface; lightly knead. Roll dough to 1/4-inch thickness; cut into squares. Fry in oil; turn once; beignets are done when golden brown, and "puffed" a little. Drain; sprinkle generously with sugar; Serve with cafe au lait. You'll feel like you are in Louisiana!!

CAFE AU LAIT

Simply combine equal amounts of hot, strong, black coffee and hot milk. Then, add sugar to taste. As simple as that!! Serve with beignets. Nothing Better!!

We thank Lucie Lee Lanoux of Alexandria, Louisiana, for this wonderful and traditional Louisiana favorite!!

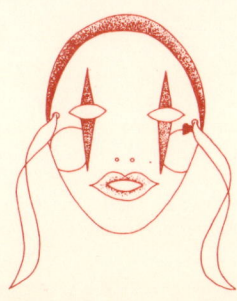

A Great Little Cajun Recipe
Just For You!

To:

MARDI GRAS CHEER

1-1/2 cups sugar
1 pt. water
1 pt. good bourbon or rum
Juice of 5 lemons
Juice of 2 oranges
Rinds of 3 lemons
Rinds of 2 oranges

Dissolve sugar in water; add rest of ingredients; refrigerate. Leave rinds in mixture overnight. Next day squeeze juice from rinds. Refrigerate 24 hours. Serve cold.
Serves 6-8. (Easily doubled, etc.)

Mardi Gras is Shrove Tuesday, the last day before Lent. This day is celebrated with a carnival. In Louisiana, the Mardi Gras season begins in January and is celebrated with parties and parades which culminate in a tremendous party in many Louisiana cities and towns on Shrove (Fat) Tuesday!

CAFE BRULOT

4 sticks cinnamon
Peel of 1 orange, broken up
Peel of 1 lemon, broken up
3-1/2 Tbsps. sugar
6 ozs. brandy
48 ozs. strong, hot, black coffee

Place first 5 ingredients in pan; heat. When brandy is hot (do NOT boil), ignite with match. Stir mixture with ladle; keep flame going 2 minutes. Pour coffee into flaming mixture; fill demitasse cups, and enjoy!!
Yields 12 4-ounce servings.

This recipe comes to us from Betty Yerger of Lake Providence, Louisiana. Cafe Brulot is a marvelous way to end a meal!!

A Great Little Cajun Recipe
Just For You!

To:

LOUISIANA'S BEST HUSH PUPPIES

1 cup cornmeal
1 tsp. baking powder
1 tsp. salt
1 tsp. sugar
1 cup flour
1 egg, beaten
3/4 cup milk
1/4 tsp. cayenne pepper
2/3 cup green onions & tops, chopped

Into bowl, sift first 5 ingredients. Separately, combine egg and milk; add to dry mixture; mix. Add rest of ingredients; mix well. Drop by spoonfuls into deep, hot fat; fry until brown. That Easy! Wonderful!!
Makes about 2 dozen.

SOUTHERN SPOON BREAD

2 cups milk
1/2 cup Cream of Wheat
1 tsp. salt
4 Tbsps. butter, cut up
1/4 tsp. cayenne pepper
1 cup Cheddar cheese, grated
1 egg, lightly beaten

Cook milk and Cream of Wheat until thick; add next 4 ingredients; remove from heat; stir until cheese is melted. Put egg in bowl; add hot mixture by spoonfuls; mix after each addition; do this for 5 spoonfuls; then, add rest of mixture; mix well. Pour into greased 1 1/2-quart casserole. Bake at 350^0 for 45 minutes.
Serves 4 deliciously!

Both these recipes are favorites of Dee's!!

A Great Little Cajun Recipe
Just For You!

To:

ACADIAN BOIL

3 lemons, quartered
7 onions, quartered
3 pods garlic
1 (1 lb., 10 oz.) box salt
1 (8 oz.) jar cayenne pepper
5 bay leaves
1 Tbsp. dill
1 Tbsp. mustard seed
1 Tbsp. all spice
20 lbs. live crawfish, 5 lbs. per person

In <u>big</u> pot, bring to boil 1-1/2 gallons water; add first 9 ingredients; boil 5 minutes; add half the crawfish; boil 10-15 minutes. Remove crawfish; add rest of crawfish; boil 10-15 minutes. Peel, and enjoy with sauce made with 2 cups catsup, 1/2 cup horseradish, 1-1/2 tablespoons lemon juice, and 1 tablespoon prepared mustard. Great!!

CREOLE SEASONING

2 Tbsps. garlic powder
3-1/2 Tbsps. onion powder
1/3 cup salt
1/4 cup black pepper, freshly ground
1/3 cup paprika
2 Tbsps. dried thyme
2 Tbsps. dried oregano
1/2 tsp. cayenne pepper

Mix well all ingredients; store in glass jar. Adds zest to roasted or grilled meat, poultry, seafood, potato and corn dishes! Easily doubled.
Yields about 1-1/2 cups.

This marvelous recipe comes to us courtesy of Dorothy Anne Millikin of Tallalah, Louisiana! She tells us the recipe can be doubled, tripled, etc.

A Great Little Cajun Recipe
Just For You!

To:

FRENCH QUARTER BEIGNETS

2 cups all purpose flour
1/2 tsp. salt
1 Tbsp. baking powder
1 tsp. ground cinnamon
1 egg, beaten well
3 Tbsps. sugar
1 cup milk
1/2 tsp. vanilla extract
Hot oil for deep frying
2 cups powdered sugar

Into bowl, sift first 4 ingredients. Separately, beat well egg with next 3 ingredients; pour into flour mixture; stir until moistened. Turn onto floured surface; lightly knead. Roll dough to 1/4-inch thickness; cut into squares. Fry in oil; turn once; beignets are done when golden brown, and "puffed" a little. Drain; sprinkle generously with sugar; Serve with cafe au lait. You'll feel like you are in Louisiana!!

CAFE AU LAIT

Simply combine equal amounts of hot, strong, black coffee and hot milk. Then, add sugar to taste. As simple as that!! Serve with beignets. Nothing Better!!

We thank Lucie Lee Lanoux of Alexandria, Louisiana, for this wonderful and traditional Louisiana favorite!!

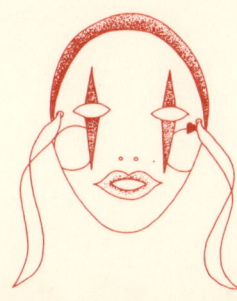

A Great Little Cajun Recipe
Just For You!

PLACE
STAMP
HERE

To:

MARDI GRAS CHEER

1-1/2 cups sugar
1 pt. water
1 pt. good bourbon or rum
Juice of 5 lemons
Juice of 2 oranges
Rinds of 3 lemons
Rinds of 2 oranges

Dissolve sugar in water; add rest of ingredients; refrigerate. Leave rinds in mixture overnight. Next day squeeze juice from rinds. Refrigerate 24 hours. Serve cold.
Serves 6-8. (Easily doubled, etc.)

Mardi Gras is Shrove Tuesday, the last day before Lent. This day is celebrated with a carnival. In Louisiana, the Mardi Gras season begins in January and is celebrated with parties and parades which culminate in a tremendous party in many Louisiana cities and towns on Shrove (Fat) Tuesday!

CAFE BRULOT

4 sticks cinnamon
Peel of 1 orange, broken up
Peel of 1 lemon, broken up
3-1/2 Tbsps. sugar
6 ozs. brandy
48 ozs. strong, hot, black coffee

Place first 5 ingredients in pan; heat. When brandy is hot (do NOT boil), ignite with match. Stir mixture with ladle; keep flame going 2 minutes. Pour coffee into flaming mixture; fill demitasse cups, and enjoy!!
Yields 12 4-ounce servings.

This recipe comes to us from Betty Yerger of Lake Providence, Louisiana. Cafe Brulot is a marvelous way to end a meal!!

A Great Little Cajun Recipe
Just For You!

To:

LOUISIANA'S BEST HUSH PUPPIES

1 cup cornmeal
1 tsp. baking powder
1 tsp. salt
1 tsp. sugar
1 cup flour
1 egg, beaten
3/4 cup milk
1/4 tsp. cayenne pepper
2/3 cup green onions & tops, chopped

Into bowl, sift first 5 ingredients. Separately, combine egg and milk; add to dry mixture; mix. Add rest of ingredients; mix well. Drop by spoonfuls into deep, hot fat; fry until brown. That Easy! Wonderful!!
Makes about 2 dozen.

SOUTHERN SPOON BREAD

2 cups milk
1/2 cup Cream of Wheat
1 tsp. salt
4 Tbsps. butter, cut up
1/4 tsp. cayenne pepper
1 cup Cheddar cheese, grated
1 egg, lightly beaten

Cook milk and Cream of Wheat until thick; add next 4 ingredients; remove from heat; stir until cheese is melted. Put egg in bowl; add hot mixture by spoonfuls; mix after each addition; do this for 5 spoonfuls; then, add rest of mixture; mix well. Pour into greased 1 1/2-quart casserole. Bake at 350⁰ for 45 minutes.
Serves 4 deliciously!

Both these recipes are favorites of Dee's!!

A Great Little Cajun Recipe
Just For You!

To:

ACADIAN BOIL

3 lemons, quartered
7 onions, quartered
3 pods garlic
1 (1 lb., 10 oz.) box salt
1 (8 oz.) jar cayenne pepper
5 bay leaves
1 Tbsp. dill
1 Tbsp. mustard seed
1 Tbsp. all spice
20 lbs. live crawfish, 5 lbs. per person

In **big** pot, bring to boil 1-1/2 gallons water; add first 9 ingredients; boil 5 minutes; add half the crawfish; boil 10-15 minutes. Remove crawfish; add rest of crawfish; boil 10-15 minutes. Peel, and enjoy with sauce made with 2 cups catsup, 1/2 cup horseradish, 1-1/2 tablespoons lemon juice, and 1 tablespoon prepared mustard. Great!!

CREOLE SEASONING

2 Tbsps. garlic powder
3-1/2 Tbsps. onion powder
1/3 cup salt
1/4 cup black pepper, freshly ground
1/3 cup paprika
2 Tbsps. dried thyme
2 Tbsps. dried oregano
1/2 tsp. cayenne pepper

Mix well all ingredients; store in glass jar. Adds zest to roasted or grilled meat, poultry, seafood, potato and corn dishes! Easily doubled.
Yields about 1-1/2 cups.

This marvelous recipe comes to us courtesy of Dorothy Anne Millikin of Tallalah, Louisiana! She tells us the recipe can be doubled, tripled, etc.

A Great Little Cajun Recipe
Just For You!

To:

WONDERFUL SMOKED DUCK AND OYSTER GUMBO

3 ducks, wild
1/2 cup butter
1/2 cup flour
1 medium green pepper, chopped
1 large onion, chopped
1 large garlic pod, minced
1/4 cup fresh parsley, chopped
1 (10 oz.) pkg. frozen cut okra or 1/2
*   lb. fresh, cut*
1 (16 oz.) can tomatoes, or 4-6 fresh
*   tomatoes, chopped*
Salt, pepper, paprika, & red pepper
*   to taste*
1 pt. fresh oysters, cleaned, rinsed, &
*   drained*
Rice, cooked

Serves 8 generously.

Smoke ducks, away from flame, on charcoal smoker using hickory chips. Keep smoker closed; cook 4 hours. Then, put ducks in a big pot; cover with water; simmer, covered, for 2-3 hours or meat almost falls from the bones. Remove bones, being sure to remove any shot; cut meat into bite-sized chunks. Strain, and reserve duck broth. Melt butter in large skillet; add flour; brown until roux is dark golden. Add pepper and onion; brown slowly; add garlic. Pour reserved broth into large pot; stir in roux mixture. Add duck meat; cook, covered, over low heat 30 minutes. Stir in parsley, and next 3 ingredients; cook slowly until okra is tender. To serve, heat to boiling; add oysters; cook until just done. Adjust seasonings; serve over rice.

A Great Little Cajun Recipe
Just For You!

To:

CAJUN COUNTRY CATFISH STEW

1/2 cup butter
1 cup onion, chopped
1/2 cup green pepper, chopped
3 garlic pods, finely chopped
3 cups fresh tomatoes, peeled &
    coarsely chopped
1/2-1 tsp. Louisiana Hot Sauce
1/2 tsp. cumin
1/2 tsp. dried whole thyme
1/2 tsp. dried oregano
Salt & pepper to taste
2 bay leaves
4-1/2 cups water
1/2 cup rice, uncooked
1 lb. catfish fillets, cut in 1-inch
    pieces
1 (10 oz.) pkg. frozen cut okra, thawed
1 lb. shrimp, shelled & cleaned

Serves 6-8.

In butter, saute next 3 ingredients until tender. Add tomatoes and next 7 ingredients; cover; simmer 20-25 minutes; stir often. Add rice and fish; stir in well; cover; simmer 15 minutes. Stir in okra; simmer 5 minutes more. Add shrimp; heat mixture to boiling; cook 1-2 minutes, stirring constantly. Remove bay leaves, serve, and enjoy!

Delicious with a tossed salad and cornbread!

A Great Little Cajun Recipe
Just For You!

To:

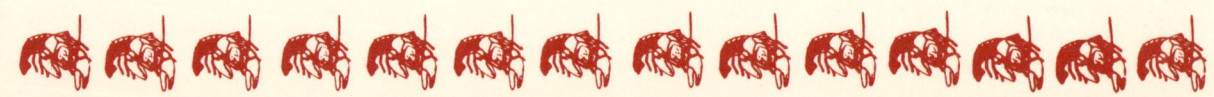

BAYOU CHICKEN JAMBALAYA

2 large yellow onions, chopped
2 pods garlic
1/4 cup butter
2 lbs. hot pork sausage, cooked &
    drained
2 (6 oz.) pkgs. long grain & wild rice
    mix, cooked per pkg.'s directions
3 Tbsps. butter
1 lb. fresh mushrooms, sliced
4 cups chicken, cooked, boned, &
    coarsely chopped
2 (2-1/4 oz.) cans sliced black olives
2 (8-1/2 oz.) cans artichoke hearts,
    drained & sliced
1/2 cup green onions & tops, chopped

Serves 8-10.

Jambalaya, a traditional dish in Louisiana, consists of rice, meat, or seafood, cooked in one pot, with garlic, onions, and other vegetables and seasonings.

In large pot, saute onions and garlic in butter until tender; add sausage and rice; mix well; cook 1 minute. Separately, in 3 Tbsps. butter, saute mushrooms; drain. To sausage/rice mixture, add mushrooms and next 3 ingredients; bake at 350° for 25 minutes; top with green onions; cook 8-10 minutes more or until completely heated. Excellent!

Many thanks to Liz Salles of Covington, Louisiana! Cooked turkey may be substituted for the chicken for a marvelous after holiday treat!

A Great Little Cajun Recipe
Just For You!

To:

PARTY SAUSAGE AND SHRIMP JAMBALAYA

6 lbs. hot link sausage, cut in
   1/2-inch pieces
2 large onions, chopped
1 cup parsley, chopped
5 pods garlic, chopped
7-1/2 cups water
1 (16 oz.) can whole tomatoes, mashed
1 tsp. thyme
Salt & pepper to taste
6 cups rice, uncooked
3 lbs. shrimp, shells removed

Serves 20-22. (Easily halved)

In large, heavy skillet, cook sausage. Add onions; let cook until onions are clear; add parsley and garlic; cook until parsley is limp, 3-5 minutes. Add water and next 3 ingredients; bring to boil; add rice and shrimp. Stir twice; put heat on low; cover. Cook until rice is tender, about 30 minutes. If cooking mixture sticks, add an additional 1/2-cup water; stir. Serve hot with French bread. Can't Be Beat!

Wonderful served on cool fall and winter evenings! We very much thank Suzanne Wood of Baton Rouge for this delicious Jambalaya!

A Great Little Cajun Recipe
Just For You!

To:

NEW ORLEANS BEST CRAWFISH CREOLE

1/2 cup onion, finely chopped
1/2 cup celery, finely chopped
2 cloves garlic, crushed
3 Tbsps. butter
1 (16 oz.) can whole tomatoes
1 (8 oz.) can tomato sauce
1-1/2 tsps. salt
1 tsp. sugar
1 Tbsp. Worcestershire sauce
1 tsp. chili powder
1/2 tsp. Louisiana Hot Sauce
1 lb. crawfish tails
1/2 cup bell pepper, chopped
2 tsps. cornstarch
2 tsps. water

Serves 6-8.

Creole refers to Louisianians of Spanish/Mediterranean descent. Creole cooking lends a Mediterranean flavor to the best of Louisiana cooking!!

Saute first 3 ingredients in butter until tender but not brown. Add tomatoes and next 6 ingredients; simmer, uncovered, 45 minutes. Add crawfish and bell pepper; cover; simmer 5 minutes. Mix cornstarch with water; add to crawfish mixture; simmer until thickened. Serve hot over rice. Outstanding And Easy One Dish Meal!!

This super recipe comes to us compliments of Louisiana's Seafood Promotion Board! You may substitute a pound of shrimp for the crawfish and create a delicious Shrimp Creole!!

*A Great Little Cajun Recipe
Just For You!*

To:

BLACKENED LOUISIANA FARM-RAISED CATFISH

2 Tbsps. paprika
2-1/2 tsps. salt
1 tsp. onion powder
1-1/2 tsps. garlic powder
2 tsps. lemon pepper
1-1/2 tsps. cayenne pepper
1 tsp. ground thyme
1 tsp. freshly ground pepper
1-1/2 tsps. basil
6 catfish fillets
2 sticks butter, melted

Serves 6.

Louisiana's Farm-Raised Catfish Industry continues to grow and prosper! Des Allemands hosts the annual Louisiana Catfish Festival in July!!

Heat large iron skillet to very hot, about 10 minutes; at same time, combine first 9 ingredients. Then, dip each fillet in butter; coat well. Using about 1 tablespoon seasoning per fillet, thoroughly coat both sides. Put fillets, 3 at a time, in hot skillet; drizzle 1 tablespoon butter over each; cook 2 minutes per side (there will be smoke which is okay!); remove cooked fillets; repeat process once. Good!!

This recipe is one of Jeanne's favorites!! You may use this recipe to successfully blacken any kind of fresh fish fillet!!!

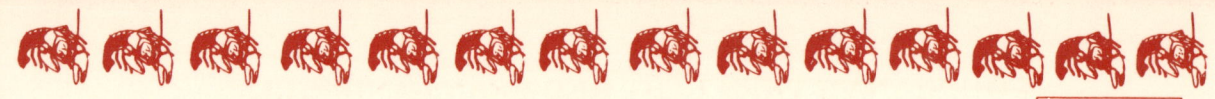

A Great Little Cajun Recipe
Just For You!

PLACE
STAMP
HERE

To:

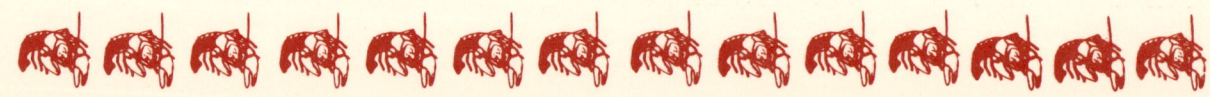

LOUISIANA'S VERY BEST RED BEANS AND RICE

1 lb. dried red beans, rinsed
1 big ham bone
2 qts. water
1-1/2 lbs. Italian sausage
2 pods garlic, minced
2 onions, chopped
3 stalks celery, chopped
2 bay leaves
Salt & pepper to taste
1 tsp. cumin
1 bunch green onions & tops,
    chopped
Rice, cooked
10 or more parsley sprigs

Serves 8-10.

In big pot, place beans and ham bone in water. Saute sausage with garlic until brown; drain; add to beans. Mix in next 5 ingredients; bring mixture to boil; turn heat to low; simmer 2-3 hours; stir occasionally. If needed, add more water to keep mixture very moist. When done, remove 1/8-cup beans; mash; return to beans; top with green onions; heat to hot. Serve over rice garnished with parsley.

This is one of Jeanne's recipes and is wonderful served to friends with hush puppies and a tossed salad!!

A Great Little Cajun Recipe
Just For You!

To:

CAJUN STEAK FINGERS

1 large round steak, trimmed of all
    fat & cut into small strips
3/4 cup all-purpose flour
2 tsps. salt
1 Tbsp. dehydrated onion
1 tsp. garlic powder
Enough black pepper to make
    mixture almost black
Enough red pepper for mixture to
    show some red
Dry flour for coating
Vegetable oil for frying

Serves 3-4. (Easily doubled)

Set steak aside. In bowl and using your hands, combine and mix well next 6 ingredients. Mix until mixture is gooey; if necessary, use small amount of water. Mixture MUST be gooey and sticky. Add steak; mix again; thoroughly cover steak strips. Cover tightly with plastic wrap; refrigerate 6-8 hours. Before cooking, roll each strip in dry flour. Fry strips in hot oil to desired "doneness".

Kathleen Drott of Pineville, Louisiana, tells us that these steak fingers are a family favorite and that venison steaks are also delicious prepared this way!!

A Great Little Cajun Recipe
Just For You!

PLACE
STAMP
HERE

To:

NEW ORLEANS BREAD PUDDING
(With Marvelous Whiskey Sauce)

*6 cups 3-day-old French bread, cut
  in 1-inch cubes*
2 cups milk
2 medium eggs
1 cup sugar
1 Tbsp. vanilla extract
1/2-3/4 cup pecans, chopped
1/4 cup raisins
1-2 Tbsps. butter
3/4 cup sugar
1/6 cup water
*1/4 cup + 2 Tbsps. butter, cut in
  pieces*
2-3 Tbsps. bourbon
1/2 tsp. cornstarch

Serves 6. (Easily doubled)

8x8-inch pan (9x13-inch pan if doubled)

*Many thanks to Ellen Reynolds of
Shreveport, Louisiana, for this super
recipe!!*

Place bread in large bowl; cover with milk; set aside 15 minutes. Separately, beat eggs, sugar, and vanilla until thick and creamy; add pecans and raisins; stir in well. Pour mixture over bread; mix well. Spoon mixture into buttered 8x8-inch pan; dot with butter; put dish in shallow pan of water; bake at 350° for 55-60 minutes or until knife inserted in center comes out clean. Let stand at room temperature 10 minutes. To make sauce, combine, in saucepan, sugar with water; bring to boil without stirring; simmer 4-5 minutes; lower heat; add butter; whisk until butter is absorbed, and mixture is creamy. Remove from heat. Separately, combine bourbon and cornstarch; stir into sauce; beat until smooth. Return to burner; whisk 1-2 minutes, just until sauce boils and bubbles. Serve warm over pudding. Wonderful!

A Great Little Cajun Recipe
Just For You!

To:

LOUISIANA CAJUN CAKE SUPREME

1/2 cup butter, softened
1-1/2 cups sugar
2 eggs
2 cups all-purpose flour
2 tsps. baking powder
1/2 tsp. baking soda
1/4 tsp. salt
1 (15-1/4 oz.) can crushed pineapple,
    drained, reserving 1/2 cup juice
1/4 cup butter
1/2 cup sugar
1/3 cup evaporated milk
1/4 cup flaked coconut
1/2 cup pecans, chopped
1/2 tsp. vanilla extract
Flaked coconut, toasted (optional)
Pineapple slices (optional)
Fresh pineapple leaves (optional)

1 Bundt pan

With electric mixer, cream 1/2-cup butter with sugar; add eggs, one at a time; beat well after each addition. Combine next 4 ingredients; add to creamed mixture, alternately with reserved juice, beginning and ending with flour mixture. Mix until just blended after each addition; stir in crushed pineapple. Pour into greased Bundt pan; bake at 350° for 50-55 minutes or tests done. Cool 10 minutes; turn onto serving plate. In saucepan, combine 1/4 cup butter and next 4 ingredients, bring to boil; reduce heat; simmer 3 minutes. Stir in vanilla; spoon on top of warm cake. Sprinkle with toasted coconut, and garnish with pineapple slices and leaves.

Jean Hurley of Lafayette, Louisiana, created this magnificent Cajun Cake! Lafayette is home to Festivals Acadiens which is held every September and features the best in Cajun music, a food festival, crafts, and entertaining folk life segments!!

A Great Little Cajun Recipe
Just For You!

To:

THREE INCREDIBLE LOUISIANA DESSERT TREATS

FROZEN CREOLE CREAM CHEESE

12 ozs. large curd cottage cheese
2 cups half & half
1 cup whipping cream
3/4 cup sugar
6 Tbsps. fresh lemon juice, strained
1 tsp. vanilla

In blender, mix cottage cheese and cup half and half until smooth; add rest of half and half and remaining ingredients; mix until smooth. Transfer to ice cream maker; process per manufacturer's instructions. Serve with Fig conserve or alone. Delicious!
Serves 8-10.

Many thanks to Julianne Lansing of New Orleans for this outstanding recipe!!

LOUISIANA BOUNCE
(Drink Your Dessert)

6 ozs. brandy
2 ozs. cream de coca
4 large scoops vanilla ice cream

In blender, mix all ingredients well. Serve in champagne glasses.
Serves 6-8 deliciously!

VERY SPECIAL PRALINES

2 cups sugar
1 cup evaporated milk
3 Tbsps. orange rind, grated
1 cup miniature marshmallows
3 cups pecan halves

Bring first 3 ingredients to hard boil; cook to soft ball stage (238° on candy thermometer); add marshmallows and pecans. Beat until thick; drop by spoonfuls onto waxed paper; cool. Good!
Yields 2 dozen.

*A Great Little Cajun Recipe
Just For You!*

To:

Great Flavors Series of Cookbooks
P. O. Box 922
Pine Bluff, Arkansas 71613

_____ copies of *A Great Little Cajun Book* at $6.95 each _____
_____ copies of *A Great Little Flavor of Texas* at $6.95 each _____
_____ copies of *Ultimate Weekly Planner* at $16.95 each _____
_____ copies of *Great Flavors of Louisiana* at $9.50 each _____
_____ copies of *Great Flavors of Mississippi* at $9.50 each _____
_____ copies of *Great Flavors of Texas* at $11.50 each _____
_____ copies of *Great Flavors of Arkansas* at $9.50 each _____
_____ copies of *More Great Flavors of Arkansas* at $9.50 each _____

Total _____

Each per copy price includes postage, handling, and tax.

Telephone your order by calling our 24-hour answering service at 1-800-874-5725.

Enclosed is my check or money order for $ _____ .
(for MasterCard or Visa charges, see back of page.)

Name _____

Street _____

City _____ *State* _____ *Zip* _____

Telephone Number _____

Charge to my: ☐   MasterCard   ☐   VISA

Account Number:

☐☐☐☐☐☐☐☐☐☐☐☐☐☐☐☐   ☐☐☐☐

Expiration Date: _____

Customer's Signature: _____

Please watch for other Southern Flavors Publications and Products!!